21st Century
Junior Library

DISCOVER THE VELOCIRAPTOR

Lucia Raatma

Our Prehistoric World: Dinosaurs

Published in the United States of America by:

CHERRY LAKE PRESS
2395 South Huron Parkway, Suite 200, Ann Arbor, Michigan 48104
www.cherrylakepress.com

Content Adviser: Gregory M. Erickson, PhD, Dinosaur Paleontologist, Department of Biological
Science, Florida State University, Tallahassee, Florida

Reading Adviser: Marla Conn, ReadAbility, Inc.

Photo and Illustration Credits: Cover: © Daniel Eskridge/Dreamstime.com; pages 5, 13: © Kitti Kahotong/
Dreamstime.com; page 6: © STT0006461/Media Bakery; page 7: © Anton Shahrai/Shutterstock.com; page 9:
© Jim Zuckerman/Alamy; page 10: © Fabio Iozzino/Dreamstime.com; pages 11, 16: © Ralf Juergen Kraft/
Shutterstock.com; page 12: © STT0006462/Media Bakery; page 14: © kamomeen/Shutterstock.com; page 19:
© frantic00/Shutterstock.com; page 20: © ZUMA Wire Service/Alamy; page 21: © diy13/Shutterstock.com

Cherry Lake Press is an imprint of Cherry Lake Publishing Group.

Library of Congress Cataloging-in-Publication Data has been filed and is available at catalog.loc.gov.

Cherry Lake Press would like to acknowledge the work of the Partnership for 21st Century Learning, a Network
of Battelle for Kids. Please visit http://www.battelleforkids.org/networks/p21 for more information.

Printed in the United States of America

Note from publisher: Websites change regularly, and their future contents are outside of our control.
Supervise children when conducting any recommended online searches for extended learning opportunities.

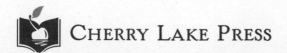

CONTENTS

WHAT WAS A VELOCIRAPTOR?

When you think of dinosaurs, do you think of huge creatures? The *Velociraptor* was not one of those! It was a fast, fairly small dinosaur. It raced along on long, thin legs. The *Velociraptor* lived about 75 million years ago. It is now **extinct**, like all other dinosaurs.

Velociraptors were made famous in the movie *Jurrassic Park*. The movie dinosaurs were 6 feet (1.8 meters) tall. They did not have feathers. Real *Velociraptors* were much different!

Velociraptor is a name that means "speedy thief." This dinosaur lived in what are now Mongolia and China. It usually lived in hot, dry areas. Its **habitat** was probably like a desert but with streams.

Scientists believe Mongolia was much warmer millions of years ago than it is now.

Look!

Find Mongolia on a map. Then research this country in books or online. What is the land like there today? What animals live there now?

WHAT DID A VELOCIRAPTOR LOOK LIKE?

Compared to other dinosaurs, the *Velociraptor* was small. It was about 6 to 7 feet (1.8 to 2.1 m) long. It stood about 3 feet (0.9 m) high. It probably weighed between 15 and 30 pounds (6.8 to 13.6 kilograms). You probably weigh more than that!

Velociraptors were much shorter than most adult humans.

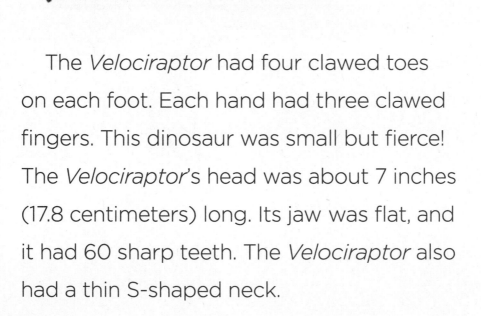

The *Velociraptor* had four clawed toes on each foot. Each hand had three clawed fingers. This dinosaur was small but fierce! The *Velociraptor*'s head was about 7 inches (17.8 centimeters) long. Its jaw was flat, and it had 60 sharp teeth. The *Velociraptor* also had a thin S-shaped neck.

One claw on each of the *Velociraptor*'s feet was much larger than the others.

Velocriaptors could not fly. But scientists believe they were related to other dinosaurs that could fly.

Scientists believe the *Velociraptor* had feathers like modern birds do. These feathers may have been very colorful. Even though it had feathers, the Velociraptor could not fly. Its short arms could not act like wings.

Think!

Think of some other feathered creatures that cannot fly. What do they use their feathers for?

Velociraptors might have hunted animals much larger than themselves.

HOW DID A VELOCIRAPTOR LIVE?

The *Velociraptor* was a **carnivore**. This **predator** used its claws to tear into its **prey**. One claw on each foot was bigger than the others. These extra-long claws were about 3.5 inches (8.9 cm) in length. They were sharp. In fact, they were the *Velociraptor*'s most important weapons.

A Velociraptor could not run quickly for very long.

Imagine seeing a *Velociraptor* running upright on two legs! Scientists believe it could run 24 miles (39 kilometers) per hour. That is as fast as some cars may drive in your neighborhood. The *Velociraptor* ran fastest in short bursts. The dinosaur's thick tail provided balance while it ran.

Make a Guess!

The next time you are in the car, make a guess. How fast are you traveling? On a highway, you may go much faster than a Velociraptor. But if you are in traffic, you may go slower.

The *Velociraptor* may have used its feathers to attract a **mate**. It might have used them to hide from attackers. The feathers may have helped it stay warm or cool off. They might have helped shelter the dinosaur from the sun. The *Velociraptor* may also have used its feathers to protect its nest of eggs.

Create!

Go outside in your yard or to a park. Draw a picture of a bird that you see. In what ways does it look like a *Velociraptor*?

Scientists are not sure what the *Velociraptor*'s feathers were for, or even what they looked like.

How have we learned about *Velociraptors*? Scientists have discovered fossils and studied them. The first *Velociraptor* fossil was found in Mongolia in 1924. Others have been found in China. One *Velociraptor* fossil was found tangled up with another dinosaur. The two had been fighting when they died. Does hunting for fossils sound exciting to you?

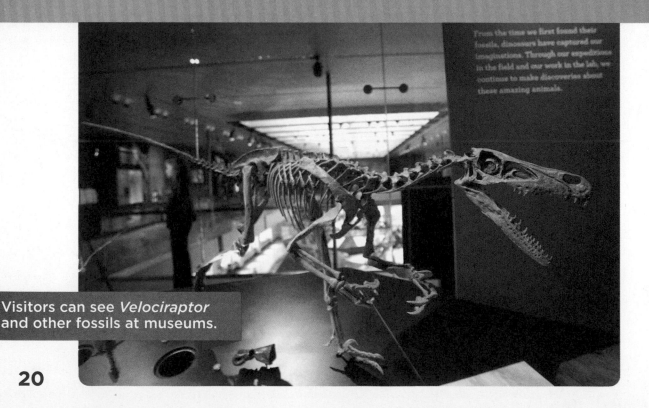

From the time we first found their fossils, dinosaurs have captured our imaginations. Through our expeditions in the field and our work in the lab, we continue to make discoveries about these amazing animals.

Visitors can see *Velociraptor* and other fossils at museums.

VELOCIRAPTOR

CRETACEOUS
MONGOLIA

TRIASSICA™
THE SPECIMEN COLLECTION OF DINOSAURS

Ask Questions!

Think about *Velociraptors* the next time you visit the zoo. Ask zoo workers questions about the animals that you see. Do they have features like the *Velociraptor*?

GLOSSARY

carnivore (KAHR-nuh-vor) an animal that eats meat

extinct (ek-STINGKT) describing a type of plant or animal that has completely died out

fossils (FAH-suhlz) the preserved remains of living things from thousands or millions of years ago

habitat (HAB-uh-tat) the place and natural conditions in which a plant or animal lives

mate (MATE) a male or female partner of a pair of animals

predator (PRED-uh-tur) an animal that lives by hunting other animals for food

prey (PRAY) an animal that is hunted by other animals for food

FIND OUT MORE

Books

Braun, Dieter. *Dictionary of Dinosaurs: An Illustrated A to Z of Every Dinosaur Ever Discovered.* New York, NY: Chartwell Books, 2022.

Rockwood, Leigh. *Velociraptor.* New York, NY: PowerKids Press, 2012.

Websites

With an adult, learn more online with these suggested searches.

National Geographic: Kids—Velociraptor
Read about the unique features of a *Velociraptor*.

Kiddle—Velociraptor Facts for Kids
Learn more about the important *Velociraptor* discoveries scientists made.

INDEX

ABOUT THE AUTHOR

Lucia Raatma has written dozens of books for young readers. She and her family live in the Tampa Bay area of Florida. They enjoy looking at the dinosaur fossils at the local science museum.